Carlton, Neth and Colwi

on old picture postcards

Grenville Jennings

**Designed and Published by
Reflections of a Bygone Age,
Keyworth, Nottingham**

Carlton Hill, Nottingham. No. 424.

1. This C. & A.G. Lewis card, showing Carlton Hill with tram no. 7 on route no. 8 (to Carlton) prominently on view, was posted to Buxton in 1926.

ISBN 0 946245 64 9

**Printed by
Adlard Print and Typesetting Services,
Ruddington, Notts.**

INTRODUCTION

The purpose of this book is to portray Carlton, Netherfield and Colwick through the medium of picture postcards, which were at the height of the popularity in Edwardian times - both as items on which to send messages and as pictures to collect.

Picture Postcards were first published in Britain in 1894, but it was not until decade later that they began to take off, when in 1902 the Post Office allowed message to be written on the address side. This meant that the whole of the other side was available for the picture, which obviously gave more scope to the publishers.

Photographic viewcards became very popular and the postcard became the most important way of communicating news or messages in much the same way as the telephone is used today. The years up to 1914 were the 'Golden Age' of picture postcard when millions of cards portraying every imaginable subject were published by a host of national and local firms. Hardly a village or hamlet was not documented at that time by a postcard publisher, though sometimes the number of cards available was unrelated to the size of a community.

The majority of cards illustrated in this book were produced by local firms which really only to be expected. The publishing giants of the age published fine cards of towns and city centres and tourist locations, but with a few exceptions - notably W.H. Smith - were reluctant to venture into the suburbs and villages.

One of the most prolific publishers of early local cards was Albert Hindley, who ran stationery shop on Clumber Street in Nottingham (currently occupied by Granada TV Rentals). He issued the "Clumber" series of postcards covering much of Nottingham and the surrounding area. These date from around 1905 and were printed in colour by a firm in Glasgow. Another local publisher well-represented on the following pages is C. & A.G. Lewis.

What is striking about many of the cards is the relatively empty streets. Some photographers obviously rounded up local children to provide some animation, but the majority of the cards highlight the atmosphere of the early part of the century, when traffic outside the bigger towns was very limited.

Postally used cards with messages on can prove both interesting and informative and the views themselves provide endless fascination. A house gone here, a railway bridge no longer there, tree-lined roads unrecognisable with the disappearance of the trees. How we take things for granted.

As the present slips into the past almost un-noticed, picture postcards are a fine reminder of how things used to be. It is hoped that the following pages will allow both young and old to wallow in a little nostalgia of early Carlton, Netherfield and Colwick.

Grenville Jennings
November 1992

Front cover: A postcard published by W.H. Bee of 93 Victoria Road, Netherfield, sent to Ilkeston in May 1912, and illustrating an animated Meadow Road, Netherfield. In the distance can be seen the blind of E.J. Cope, butcher, of 40 Victoria Road.
Back cover: (top) Plenty of activity on this 1905 "Clumber" series card of Carlton crossing.
(bottom) Chandos Street, Netherfield, with the Baptist Chapel to the left. The card was posted to Loughborough in July 1910.

2. Another view of Carlton Hill by Lewis dating from 1926. Pedestrians stroll unconcernedly in the road as the only sign of transport is a tram.

3. Main Road, Carlton, on an anonymously-published card of about 1906.

4. Another C. & A.G. Lewis card (no. 758), showing the tram terminus in Carlton. This particular service began in 1910, was extended in 1914, and finally closed in March 1932. On the right is the 'Earl of Chesterfield' public house.

Terminus, Carlton. No. 758.

5. An almost deserted Main Street, Carlton, on a card by Nottingham publisher Spree in the 1920s.

6. The writer of this "Rex" series postcard, sent to Miss Frost at Sheffield in 1938 (though it was published some twelve years earlier) advises *"this is a view of Conway Road: our avenue turns off it; the house is among the trees. I have put a cross about where it is."*

232   MANOR ROAD, CARLTON.

7. Centre of attraction on this W.H. Smith-published card of Manor Road is the horse and cart passing the fire station. Card posted to Derby in January 1915.

8. Anonymously-published card of Orlando Drive, Carlton, sent to Birmingham in August 1913. All the children in the picture have hats on.

9. The grocery store of Alfred George on the corner of Willow Road. *"Lottie ar George took us to the arboretum last night. It was after 9 before we got home. We ca come back on the tram to Carlton - they have started to go to Carlton now so it make it better,"* wrote a loving daughter to her mother in Loughborough in July 1914 - for days before the first world war started.

10. Carlton Library and Fire Station on Manor Road *(see also illus. 7)*. The latter wa: built in 1906 at a cost of £500 to house one manual engine and fire escape. As ofter happened, a large crowd of children is eager to be part of the photographer's work. A horse and trap, two bicycles, and a motor-car form the traffic on the street, on which horse droppings are plentiful. Postcard sent to Keighley in July 1914.

11. Midland Road, Carlton, with the road in very poor condition. On the reverse, Frank advises *"I've been called up and have to report myself on June 20th."* He posted it to Miss Duffield (Dearest May) in Woolwick on 5th June 1916 - did he survive the war?

12. Carnegie Library, Carlton, opened in 1906 at an approximate cost of £2,000. "Clumber" series no. 313.

13. St. Paul's Church, Carlton, featured on a C. & A. G. Lewis card no. 762, postally used in September 1920. The church, built in the style of the Roman Basilica, was par-'tially built in 1885 at a cost of £4,500 and completed (including fittings) in 1891 for a further £5,500.

14. The Rectory at Carlton on a 1920s postcard published by Spree. The living in 1903, gifted by the Earl of Carnarvon, was worth £350 net.

15. Another Spree card, showing Dr. Park's Corner.

317.   *Gedling Road. Carlton, Nottingham.*

16. Gedling Road, Carlton, on W.H. Smith postcard no. 317, with the local children this time apparently recruited by the photographer on an empty road (though there is a horse and cart in the background) to add interest. The card was used as a birthday greeting in December 1926.

BURTON ROAD, CARLTON, NOTTS.

17. Burton Road in Edwardian days portrayed on "Clumber" series card no. 397p, sent to Erith in April 1908.

18. Anonymously-published card of c.1910 vintage giving another view of Burton Road.

THE "ROYAL OAK,"
CARLTON NOTTS

19. The "Royal Oak" on Burton Road about 1912.

20. Station Road Corner, Carlton, with W.G. Parbery's ladies and children's outfitters' shop in the background. The writer of this card, posted to Handsworth in July 1913, advised of his arrival at New Street Station, Birmingham, the following Saturday morning.

21. A rather rural view of Saville's Crossing, Carlton. *"This is where that little girl go killed the other week by the train,""* advised Kate writing to Mabel in Alfreton in August 1907.

22. Partly as a result of the incident referred to above, a new bridge was built. Anonymously-published card showing the transition.

23. Posted at Netherfield in May, 1907, this postcard shows the crossing over the Midland Railway line from Nottingham to Newark and Lincoln. Around this time some 16 trains in each direction stopped at Carlton and Netherfield station (to the right of the crossing).

24. It's the start of the Great War in August 1914, and the station at Carlton and Netherfield is crowded with soldiers off to join the British Expeditionary Force.

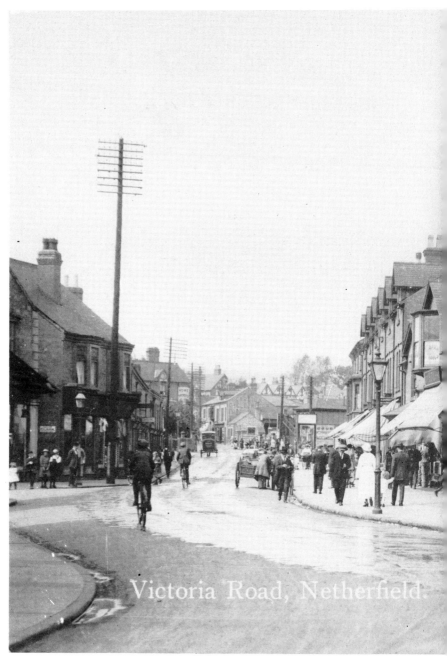

Victoria Road, Netherfield.

25. The end of Victoria Road, Netherfield, looking t
have captured a superb early 1920s moment in time
S. Smith's Shoe Booth.

Crossing. Postcard publishing firm C. & A. G. Lewis
hoppers in evidence. Among the shops on the right is

26. A fine multi-view postcard by W.H. Smith. Each view - Manor Road, Burton Road, Victoria Road, Carlton Crossing, Colwick station and Gedling Road - could be purchased as a separate card.

27. Victoria Road, Netherfield, with the Netherfield Laundry on the immediate left. Further on are the shops of Starbuck and Son, tailors, and tobacconist W.G. Barnham. *"I am sending you a view of the road in which I am staying"*, wrote Susie to a friend in Fakenham in September 1913.

28. The Star Tea Co. could be found on the corner of Curzon Street and Victoria Road, Netherfield. This postcard shows the staff outside the well-stocked shop about 1903. The shop to the right is that of George Barringham, confectioner.

29. A lovely snapshot of life on Victoria Road in 1912. Prams, a dog, assorted children, and an old lady in a bathchair all help to make up a lively scene, conducted without interference from road traffic.

30. A much later (c. 1953) view of the same road, still with a surprising absence of motor traffic.

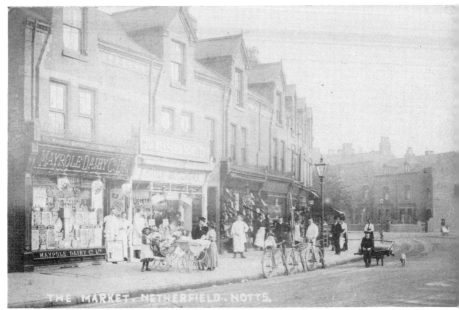

31. The Maypole Dairy Co. and Jas. Nelson - family butchers - are prominent on this card of the Market, Netherfield, sent to Gainborough in February 1911.

32. Meadow Road, Netherfield, on a "Peveril" series card, Smiths Cash Stores is on the left of the picture behind the group of boys.

33. Ashwell Street, Netherfield, and the Primitive Methodist Chapel.

34. A view of 1915 vintage further along the same street.

35. Chandos Street at its junction with Victoria Road, on a card posted in January 1918.

CEYLON TEA STORES,

NETHERFIELD, NOTTINGHAM.

36. Postcards were used as an advertising medium, as on this card of the Ceylon Tea Stores, seen to the left of the previous illustration. It was used in 1905 to send instructions to a carrier in Warwick.

37. The Baptist Chapel on the left of this picture of Chandos Street has as its pastor in 1910 the Rev. C.J. Chamberlain. This particular card was postally used four years later.

38. Netherfield Church of St. George, built in 1887 at a cost of £2,610, seen here on a "Clumber" series postcard no. 214. *"I shall not want you tomorrow, for I am not at home,"* wrote N.J. Wilson of 39 Chandos Street to Gladys Makins of Woodborough Road, Mapperley. The vicarage, to the left, cost as much to build as the church, and the living had a net yearly value of £300 in 1902, provided by the Earl of Carnarvon. Note the croquet lawn!

39. A National Union of Railwaymen's rally on Victoria Road, Netherfield, at the rear of the Railway Hotel, about 1912.

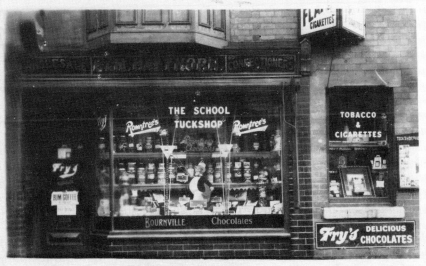

THE RIGHT SHOP — THE TUCK SHOP.
MEADOW RD., NETHERFIELD

40. E.M. Haythorn styled his confectioners' shop on Meadow Road, Netherfield, as 'The School Tuckshop' and used a postcard to advertise his premises. Bournville, Rowntree's, and Fry's are all featured, and there is a marvellous array of sweet jars in the window! The card is probably of mid-1920s vintage.

41. No indication of who published this card of the Bank Buildings, Netherfield. Lloyds Bank is centre and left, giving its name to the complex, while on the right are the shops of A. Smith (tobacconist and confectioner) and Welch the draper.

42. Some confusion over the name of this Great Northern railway station, captioned here as 'Colwick' on this "Clumber" series card no. 12. Bradshaw's Railway Guide referred to it as 'Netherfield' but the term 'Colwick and Netherfield' was generally used to distinguish it from its Midland neighbour. The card was posted from Carlton in December 1908.

43. Colwick Vale Congregational Church was built at a cost of £1,000 and opened in 1907.

44. An unusual view of Colwick Vale about 1910.

45. Though captioned 'Meadow Road, Netherfield', this C. & A. G. Lewis postcard is fact of Colwick Vale.

46. The bursting of its banks by the River Trent meant that flooding was a regula occurence for the residents of Colwick (as, indeed, it was for people in West Bridgfor and the Meadows) before the city council undertook major dredging operations. Thi card shows Colwick Vale flooded in December 1910.

7. Another view of the floods of the same month, with gardens totally under water and sheds half-submerged.

48. This "Clumber" series postcard of the Great Northern Line through Colwick Vale about 1907 exudes an air of Edwardian tranquility, with a passenger train travelling towards Nottingham.

49. Colwick crossing in 1914, featuring a good cross-section of early twentieth century transport. Card posted from Netherfield to an address in Hyson Green.

50. This photographic card, issued by the Locomotive Publishing Co., shows the Great Northern Railway yard at Colwick about 1912, with a breakdown train pulled by 0-8-2 engine no. 139 in the centre of the picture.

51. The G.N.R. Relief Fund Committee pose at Colwick, possibly during the general strike of 1926.

52. Tram no. 79 at the tram terminus, Colwick, about 1922, with a car on the no.4 service destined for Basford. Postcard published by C. & A.G. Lewis and posted to York in June 1923.

53. Another view on the no.4 Basford-Colwick route, this time in the "Rex" series, and showing tram no. 110. The photo is of mid 1920s vintage.

Old Colwick Village, Notts.

54. A somewhat uninspiring view of old Colwick village on "Clumber" card no.210, posted at Carlton in August 1908.

Colwick Park Hotel, Nottingham.

5. Colwick Hall stands half-a-mile from Colwick itself, near the River Trent, and has for many years served as both hotel and restaurant. In 1831 it suffered an attack from the Nottingham Parliamentary Reform rioters, as a result of which the death of Mrs Musters, sole heiress to the ancient family of Chaworth, was allegedly hastened. This card was published by the London firm Wrench and posted from Nottingham in July 1905.

De Lessops Monoplane in Colwick Park, Nottm. Oct 1st 1910.

56. De Lessops' monoplane at Colwick Park on 1st October 1910. Paul De Lessops, son of the Suez Canal engineer. got lost when flying from Lichfield to Burton-on-Trent and landed at Colwick Park on 30th September. This postcard was published anonymously.

57. Colwick Race Course about 1905 on "Clumber" series card no. 87. 'Wild Fox' is the horse passing the finishing line first in this race.

58. Colwick Northern Cricket Club (a railway side), winners of the Mowatt Cup in 1908.